P9-CDC-483

**BEEGHLY LIBRARY**

RAYMOND R. STAYER

ENDOWMENT

# Planet Hunter

## Geoff Marcy and the Search for Other Earths

### Vicki Oransky Wittenstein

BOYDS MILLS PRESS
Honesdale, Pennsylvania

*For Andy, the center of my universe*
—V.O.W.

## Acknowledgments

I am deeply grateful to Dr. Geoffrey W. Marcy, who invited me to the W. M. Keck Observatory in Hawaii and patiently taught me about planet hunting. He has always been available to answer my nonstop questions, even from remote locations around the world. His compelling story inspired me to write this book.

Special thanks to Dr. Debra Fischer for her expertise on many topics and for kindly agreeing to read and comment on the manuscript.

The following scientists were also generous with their time and expertise: Dr. David Bennett, University of Notre Dame; Dr. Paul Butler, Carnegie Institution of Washington; Dr. David Charbonneau, Harvard-Smithsonian Center for Astrophysics; Dr. Kevin P. Hand, NASA Jet Propulsion Laboratory; Dr. Jennifer Heldmann, NASA Ames Research Center; Dr. Carolyn Porco, Cassini Imaging Team; and Dr. Dirk Schulze-Makuch, Washington State University.

Thanks also to Koa Rice, Hawaiian outreach and cultural specialist, and to the people at Keck, especially Sarah Anderson, senior engineering assistant; observing assistants Jason McIlroy and Cynthia Wilburn; and Ashley Yeager, public information officer. Sarah Anderson bundled me in warm clothing and drove me to the summit of Mauna Kea. Her assistance, friendship, and beautiful photographs were invaluable.

I especially want to thank Andy Boyles, my editor, adviser, and friend, whose love of science and enthusiasm for the topic guided me through every step of this project.

I am grateful to my husband, Andy; my family, Ted, Alyssa, Amanda, and Jeff; and my mom, Millicent Nathan, all of whom cheered me on along the way. I also want to acknowledge my writing friends Diana, Kekla, Kitsy, and Susan, as well as my Vermont College teachers and my classmates Barb, Debbie, Rose, Tami, and Zu.
—V.O.W.

Text copyright © 2010 by Vicki O. Wittenstein
All rights reserved

Boyds Mills Press, Inc.
815 Church Street
Honesdale, Pennsylvania 18431
Printed in the United States of America

Library of Congress Cataloging-in-Publication Data

Wittenstein, Vicki O.
  Planet hunter : Geoff Marcy and the search for other Earths / Vicki O. Wittenstein.
    p. cm.
  Includes bibliographical references and index.
  ISBN 978-1-59078-592-8 (hardcover : alk. paper)
  1. Extrasolar planets. 2. Life on other planets. 3. Marcy, Geoff.  I. Title.
  QB820.W58 2010
  523.2'4—dc22

                    2009024480
First edition
The text of this book is set in 13-point Adobe Garamond.

10 9 8 7 6 5 4 3 2 1

## Image Credits

Cover illustration, page 33, Artist's concept, 70 Virginis b and Moons: © Lynette Cook.

Cover photograph, Geoff Marcy: © Laurie Hatch.

Back cover, pages 28–29, 46–47, Artist's concept, 55 Cancri and planets: Courtesy NASA/JPL-Caltech.

Pages 1, 32, and (background) 10, 20, 25, 26–27, 30, 31, 37, 41, 42, Artist's concept, 51 Pegasi comparison: © Lynette Cook.

Page 1, Geoff Marcy, control room, Keck Headquarters: Sarah Anderson.

Pages 2–3, 12–13, Artist's concept, Binary Sun: Don Dixon/cosmographica.com.

Pages 4–5, Keck Observatory at sunset: Courtesy W. M. Keck Observatory.

Pages 6–7, 8, Mauna Kea; Keck I telescope in dome; Geoff Marcy, control room, Keck Headquarters; Jason McIlroy, control room, Keck Observatory: Sarah Anderson.

Page 8, Paul Butler, Keck Observatory: Courtesy Paul Butler.

Page 9, Debra Fischer, Lick Observatory: © Laurie Hatch.

Page 10, Astronomer Omen Tablet, front and back: Courtesy Yale Babylonian Collection.

Page 10, Farnese Atlas: Courtesy E. C. Krupp, Griffith Observatory.

Page 11, Keck I mirror: Courtesy W. M. Keck Observatory.

Page 11, Earth: Courtesy Apollo 17. NASA/Goddard Space Flight Center Scientific Visualization Studio.

Page 14, Geoff Marcy as a young boy: By Morrie Camhi, courtesy Geoff Marcy.

Page 14, Gloria and Robert Marcy: Courtesy Geoff Marcy.

Page 15, Geoff Marcy at the University of Santa Cruz: Courtesy Geoff Marcy.

Page 15, Geoff Marcy, Mt. Wilson Observatory: Courtesy Douglas Carr Cunningham.

Page 15, Geoff Marcy and Susan Kegley: Courtesy Geoff Marcy.

Page 16, Geoff Marcy, Keck's Visiting Scientist Quarters: Sarah Anderson.

Page 17, Artist's concept, CoKu Tau 4 and planet: Courtesy NASA/JPL-Caltech/R. Hurt (SSC).

Pages 18 and (background) 8-9, 48, Artist's concept, transiting planet: NASA, ESA, and G. Bacon (STScl).

Pages 20–21, Graphic of Doppler shift; iodine spectrum: Courtesy Geoff Marcy.

Page 22, Geoff Marcy, control room, Keck Headquarters; High Resolution Echelle Spectrometer (HIRES): Sarah Anderson.

Page 23, Diagram of spectrometer: Terry Smith and Vicki O. Wittenstein.

Page 23, Doppler shifts during star orbit: Courtesy Geoff Marcy.

Page 23, Debra Fischer observing star spectra: © Laurie Hatch. The solar image on the computer screen was created by N.A. Sharp, NOAO/NSO/Kitt Peak FTS/AURA/NSF.

Page 24, Globular cluster NGC 6397: Courtesy NASA and The Hubble Heritage Team (STScI/AURA); Acknowledgement: A. Cool (SFSU).

Page 25, Artist's concept, transiting planet: NASA, ESA, and A. Feild (STScI).

Page 25, Chart of Sun's movement: Courtesy Geoff Marcy.

Page 25, Diagram of microlensing: Terry Smith and Vicki O. Wittenstein.

Page 26, Artist's concept, habitable zone around 55 Cancri: Courtesy NASA/JPL-Caltech.

Page 27, *Leonaspis* trilobite: Courtesy Dr. Mark S. Marshall.

Page 30, Planetary disk: Courtesy NASA/JPL-Caltech.

Page 31, Piano: Vicki O. Wittenstein, with thanks to Francesca Blood.

Page 34, Artist's concept, comparison of 55 Cancri system: Courtesy NASA/JPL-Caltech.

Page 35, Graphic of Gliese 436 b: Courtesy Dr. Jason Wright.

Page 36, Artist's concept, CoRoT-7 b: ESO/L. Calcada.

Page 37, Artist's concept, oxygen and carbon in exoplanet atmosphere: ESA and Alfred Vidal-Madjar (Institut d'Astrophysique de Paris, CNRS, France).

Pages 38–39, Photograph of Fomalhaut b: NASA, ESA, Paul Kalas (UC Berkeley).

Page 40, Artist's concept, Kepler: Courtesy NASA/Ames Research Center.

Page 40, Artist's concept, SIM: Courtesy NASA/JPL-Caltech.

Page 41, Radio telescope, Arecibo Observatory: Courtesy of the NAIC – Arecibo Observatory, a facility of the NSF. Photo by David Parker.

Page 42, Artist's concept, Venus surface: Don Dixon/cosmographica.com.

Page 43, *Kuahu Lele*, Hawaiian altar: Sarah Anderson.

Page 44, Galaxy NGC 1232: Courtesy ESO.

# Contents

Curr
QB
820
.W58
2010

4

# ONE

## Hunting for Planets like Earth

### W. M. Keck Observatory, Hawaii

As the sun sets on the summit of Mauna Kea, a dormant volcano on the Big Island of Hawaii, golden light bathes the huge domes anchoring each end of a narrow white building. A halo of orange, pink, and magenta swirls overhead, while below, waves of clouds form a blanket so thick and wide that it looks like an ocean.

The weather on the shore is hot and humid. But here at almost fourteen thousand feet above sea level, temperatures rapidly drop below 20 degrees Fahrenheit, even in the summer. No trees or plants grow on the rounded hills. Coffee-colored lava and gray cinder cover the mountaintop and crunch underfoot as workers arrive. Except for the occasional howl of the wind, all is silent.

*Sunset at the Keck Observatory on top of Mauna Kea.*

*Gentle hills (in the background, at right) dot the remote summit of Mauna Kea. They are known as* pu'u *in Hawaiian. Some are important cultural landmarks named for Hawaiian goddesses.*

When the sky begins to darken, a loud buzzer warns any technicians walking on the decks and catwalks inside the domes. A motor drones as the top and bottom shutters of one of the domes open. The dome rotates, rumbling like a train as its steel wheels roll along a track at the base. One of the twin telescopes at the W. M. Keck Observatory points to the stars. The night's viewing is about to begin.

Farther down the mountain, about two thousand feet above sea level, lies the W. M. Keck Observatory Headquarters. From there, astronomers can operate the telescope, using a real-time video connection between headquarters and the observatory. Tonight, Dr. Geoffrey W. Marcy, an astronomer who hunts for planets, is at headquarters. Jason McIlroy, an observing assistant, mans the telescope on the summit.

Mist hides the sky from headquarters, but Geoff Marcy isn't worried. He studies a computer screen that details the weather conditions at the summit. "Wow, the viewing is excellent, Jason," Marcy says into a microphone.

The Keck I telescope peers through the dome opening into the starry night. The Keck I and Keck II telescopes are the largest twin optical telescopes in the world. Marcy uses the Keck I.

Astronomers like Marcy no longer look directly through a telescope eyepiece. Instead, a device similar to a digital camera records the image in the telescope. The image is transmitted to computers for analysis.

*Jason McIlroy operates the telescope at the summit. McIlroy and Marcy can see each other by video as they work. Marcy is shown in the monitor above McIlroy's desk.*

## Planet Hunter: Paul Butler

Dr. Paul Butler hunted planets with Geoff Marcy for years. With their team, they found about half of the known extrasolar planets.

"What I love about planet hunting are the challenges of improving the system," Butler says. "I also love looking at the stars and knowing that many have planets that I have found. I am especially proud of the fact that I have never made a false planet claim."

Butler figured out how to use iodine gas to sharpen measurements of star movement, which made planet detection possible. He also helped develop the computer software that analyzes the measurements and pinpoints wobbling stars. Planet-hunting groups across the world now use this detection system. In late 2007, Butler and Dr. Steven Vogt, the designer and builder of the spectrometers at the Keck and Lick observatories, formed their own planet search team.

"I love the fact that with glass, steel, and silicon chips, in effect rocks and sand, we have put together a system that can find planets around stars that are light-years away," he says.

The time is almost 7:00 p.m., the beginning of Marcy's block of time to use the telescope. A long night of planet hunting stretches ahead. He will finish at 5:30 in the morning. For the next three days, Marcy will sleep during the day, play tennis late in the afternoon, eat a quick dinner, and then go to the telescope control room at 7:00 p.m. He keeps his fingers crossed that the good weather will hold. Telescope time is costly, and the instrument is sensitive. When the weather is bad, the telescope shuts down for the night.

## Intelligent Life Beyond Our Solar System?

Tonight, Marcy is excited: maybe he will find another distant planet orbiting a star like our Sun. Maybe this time the planet will be similar to Earth—the kind of planet most likely to sustain life.

Since 1995, Marcy, Dr. Paul Butler, and their co-workers have discovered or helped to discover 180 of the 400 planets found outside our solar system, which are known as extrasolar planets. Dr. Debra Fischer, a key member of the team, helps analyze the collected data. As the team develops more and more precise search techniques, Marcy comes closer to his dream of finding a small, rocky, Earth-like planet, one that might harbor life. In 2006, the team announced one of the smallest planets discovered so far. This planet, which orbits the star Gliese 876, is about six times more massive than Earth. The planet might seem large, but most of the known extrasolar planets are even bigger. They are about three hundred times more massive than Earth, which puts them in a class with Jupiter and Saturn.

More recent discoveries have been equally thrilling. In 2007, for the first time, astronomers determined the composition of an extrasolar planet by figuring out the planet's density. This planet, which orbits the star Gliese 436, is made of rock and water, similar to our Earth. Later that year, Marcy's team announced their finding of a fifth planet orbiting the star 55 Cancri, the first time five extrasolar planets have been discovered orbiting one star. As of this writing, the structure of this planetary system is the closest we know of to our own solar system. And new planetary systems are being discovered all the time, by Marcy's team and by others.

"Is the Earth a one-in-a-thousand shot, a one-in-a-million shot?" Marcy wonders. He adjusts the controls on one of the fourteen computers that line the wall of the telescope control room. "Surely in this huge universe there are other planets that have conditions ripe for life. But are there ten in the Milky Way galaxy? A billion? Or is there only one, our Earth? And if there's a planet like Earth, how likely is it to have intelligent life?"

Stars and planets are continually forming in the universe. Marcy estimates that of the two hundred billion stars in our Milky Way galaxy, about 10 percent, or 20 billion, have planetary systems. About one quarter, or five billion, of these planetary systems probably have a rocky planet like Earth, ripe for life. That means there could be billions of Earth-like planets in our galaxy. Let's suppose, conservatively, that intelligent species live on only one Earth-like planet in a million. According to Marcy, the Milky Way then would have thousands of advanced civilizations.

Questions like these spurred Marcy to begin hunting for planets in 1985. At the time, some scientists thought other planets might lie outside our solar system, but no one had ever found one. Marcy wanted evidence. With Butler's help, Marcy refined and adapted a detection method, called Doppler spectroscopy. They worked for ten years to find their first planet.

## The Journey to Discovery

Before 1999, Keck Observatory had no video connection between the telescope on the summit and headquarters below. Marcy and Butler had to drive to the top of Mauna Kea several times a year to use the telescope. Getting there wasn't easy. The road to the summit is mostly dirt and without guardrails. The road freezes over with ice and snow. Near the top, a series of S curves are so sharp and steep that a wrong move could send a four-wheel-drive vehicle hurtling over the side of the mountain. At night, the descent can be even more harrowing,

**Planet Hunter: Debra Fischer**

Dr. Debra Fischer analyzed the data that revealed three Jupiter-size planets orbiting the star Upsilon Andromedae. Her examination of star movements was crucial in the discovery of 55 Cancri f, the fifth planet orbiting the star 55 Cancri. Since then, she and her colleague Jeff Valenti have analyzed more than one thousand stars. They hope to learn more about how planets form.

The Upsilon Andromedae system held surprises. The first planet lies so close to the star that it completes an orbit in only four days. The second and third planets are about as far from their star as Venus and Mars are from the Sun. "I realized at a gut level that the process of forming planets must be easier than scientists had appreciated before," Fischer says. "How else could three Jupiter-size planets be crammed into the inner part of the Upsilon Andromedae system?"

Fischer is also hunting for Earth-like planets around the stars Alpha Centauri A and B, a double-star system and our closest neighbor. Says Fischer, "If you ever want to travel to another star system—too hard now!—this would be a likely destination."

*Many ancient astronomers recorded their observations of the sky on stone or clay tablets, using a type of writing known as cuneiform. Diviners, who tried to predict the future, also recorded omens and forecasts based on astronomical events. The front and back sides of the tablet above, most likely written by diviners around 550 B.C., give examples of specific stars an observer might see on a given night, and discuss what it means if the star is seen.*

## Stars and Planets Have Many Names

Many common star names come from ancient languages, especially Arabic. Modern astronomers use a system for naming stars that was devised in the 1600s. A star is called by a Greek letter followed by the name of its constellation. The brightness of the star determines the letter. For example, the brilliant star commonly known as Vega (from the Arabic word *Wega*) is named Alpha Lyrae. *Alpha* is the first letter in the Greek alphabet, and Alpha Lyrae is the brightest star in the constellation Lyra. Astronomers have run out of Greek letters and developed other ways to name stars. Newly detected stars might be named for those who discovered them, those who cataloged them, or the star's location. Some other names for Vega are 3Lyr, HR7001, and HD172167.

For extrasolar planets, the star's name goes first, followed by a lowercase letter for the planet. The planets are named in the order they are discovered. For example, the first planet detected orbiting the star 55 Cancri is known as 55 Cancri *b*, the second and third are 55 Cancri *c* and *d*, and so on to *f*, the fifth and most recent discovery. (There is no *a*.)

*In 129 B.C., the Greek astronomer Hipparchus wrote a catalog of the stars. The catalog was lost for centuries until 2005, when Dr. Bradley E. Schaefer, a professor at Louisiana State University, discovered that the catalog was reproduced on a Roman statue called the Farnese Atlas, above. On the globe is a map of the constellations in the Western sky as described in Hipparchus's catalog.*

since headlights are not allowed above the eleven-thousand-foot level. Any light can distort the telescope measurements. Working long hours on the summit is difficult, too. The air is so thin that many people become nauseated and dizzy. Some use oxygen tanks and masks to breathe easier.

Now, Marcy rarely goes to the summit. In fact, he doesn't even have to go to Hawaii to observe anymore. Recently, a remote video connection to Keck from the University of California, Berkeley (UC Berkeley), allows him to observe while staying close to his home. He recalls the first time he was able to view from the lower altitude of the control room at headquarters in Waimea. "Finally, we can observe—with air!" he jokes.

But when Marcy talks about the summit of Mauna Kea, his voice warms. "Mauna Kea is precious to astronomers," he says. As in Hawaiian culture, where the goddess of Mauna Kea, *Poli'ahu*, is worshiped because of her closeness to the heavens, astronomers revere the mountain as a gateway to the universe. With the Keck I telescope, one of the most powerful optical telescopes in the world, this remote spot is one of the best planet-hunting locations on Earth.

Marcy doesn't detect extrasolar planets while he actually uses the telescope. The discovery occurs much later, after Marcy and his team have charted a star's movement and analyzed the data collected from years of observations.

"As a scientist, I want to be 100 percent certain before announcing a new planet," Marcy says. "For example, colleagues can say, 'How can you be absolutely sure there is a large planet like Jupiter out there?' Well, Jupiter takes twelve years to orbit the Sun. That means we have to chart a Jupiter-like planet for at least twelve years, plus some more, to verify that the planet is repeating its orbit." Despite the challenges of planet hunting, Marcy keeps searching. "Ultimately, you have to be passionate and really care about the planets," he says. "You are trying to do something that is part of you, as well as something great for the rest of the world."

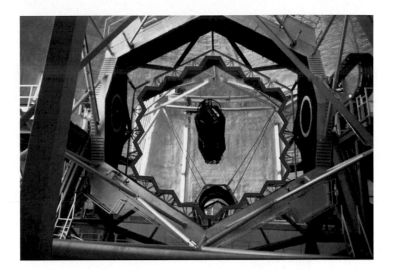

*Each Keck telescope weighs roughly three hundred tons and is as tall as an eight-story building. The primary mirror in each is made up of thirty-six individual glass hexagons coated with a thin film of shiny aluminum. The hexagons form one large reflective surface, thirty-three feet across—about the length of a large school bus. Above, the giant lens has been outlined in red.*

*Somewhere in the Milky Way galaxy, a rocky planet similar to Earth may be orbiting a Sun-like star. It may even harbor life.*

# TWO

## A Rooftop Telescope and a Dream

Los Angeles, California

When Geoff Marcy was fourteen years old, his parents bought him a small used telescope. Geoff searched for an unobstructed viewing place, a spot he could call his own. He pulled the screen out of his bedroom window and then climbed onto a flat roof over the backyard patio. He set up the telescope and focused. There, unfolding before his eyes, lay the wonders of the universe. Geoff climbed onto the patio roof almost every night. "I could see Saturn and its rings!" he recalls. "I could predict where Titan would be in its orbit around Saturn without even looking at it." Soon Geoff was hooked on outer space.

*When Geoff Marcy was young, he dreamed of planets that might look like this. This imaginary planet has two suns.*

*Geoff Marcy, age five.*

*Marcy's parents, Robert and Gloria Marcy, in 1984.*

The year was 1969, during the space age. The United States and the Soviet Union were locked in fierce competition over the development of their space programs. Geoff and his family lived in a suburb of Los Angeles, in the San Fernando Valley of California. "I remember my mom and dad waking me early in the mornings to see the Gemini and Apollo spacecraft launches," he says. "I watched Neil Armstrong hop off a ladder onto the surface of the Moon! We couldn't believe that humans were venturing into space."

Geoff's father, Robert Marcy, was a mechanical engineer who designed jet engines. Robert Marcy often brought home photographs of the jets and aircraft he was building. "The jets that flew at supersonic speeds were neat," Marcy recalls. In the 1970s, Geoff was especially thrilled by the space shuttle, since his father helped build its auxiliary

power system. "My dad's main influence on me was to emphasize the value of math and the value of being careful and thoughtful in scientific work," Marcy says.

Geoff's mother, Gloria Marcy, was an elementary-school teacher who had studied anthropology in college. She taught Geoff about the australopithecines, early humans who lived on the east African savanna. She explained how they survived against the saber-toothed tigers. "I can remember trying to imagine what it must have been like to live there in those times, two million years ago," Marcy says.

In high school, Geoff played the cello. He competed in junior varsity tennis and ran on the track team. He often invited friends up to the roof of his house to gaze at the planets and moons in our solar system. Schoolwork, though, was a struggle. "I took honors math and dropped out after a year because it was too hard. Once during a test, I froze up and had to tell the teacher I couldn't do any of the problems," he says.

As a student at UC Berkeley, Geoff continued to play the cello, learned the harpsichord, and played intramural sports. He spent most of his time, though, studying in the library. Geoff couldn't decide whether to study physics or astronomy, so he majored in both. "I remember thinking that astronomy was the study of everything in the universe and throughout all time. It encompassed the australopithecines, the baroque music composers that I loved, and the twinkling lights in the sky. And physics explained all of it, including the complicated circuitry of our amazing human brains."

In an astronomy class, Geoff had to calculate the orbit of a comet—without a calculator. "My professor taught me how predictable the universe is,"

*Marcy, age 21.*

*While Marcy was at the Carnegie Institution of Washington in Pasadena, California, he used to practice his cello inside the nearby Mount Wilson Observatory. "The acoustics in the dome are marvelous," he says.*

*Geoff and his wife, Susan, together at home.*

*Marcy outside Keck's Visiting Scientist Quarters, ready to play tennis.*

he says. "But the thousand or so calculations took me a week. If I made even one mistake, I would have to start all over."

Another professor admonished Geoff when he struggled to finish an experiment. Marcy recalls: "He said, 'If the universe can do it, so can you.'"

Marcy graduated from college with honors in 1976 and decided to become an astronomer. He then studied at the University of California, Santa Cruz, where he received his Ph.D. in astronomy and astrophysics in 1982. Some astronomers, though, criticized his Ph.D. research. Marcy started to lose confidence. He doubted whether he was smart enough to be a scientist.

Marcy received a post-graduate fellowship from the Carnegie Institution of Washington in Pasadena, California. While he was there, he worked at the Mount Wilson and Mount Palomar observatories and also at Las Campanas Observatory in Chile. Still, Marcy grew more depressed. He was intimidated by

other astronomers at the observatories who seemed to accomplish more than he did.

"One day, I was taking a shower, and as the water ran over me, I thought, 'Now wait, I've got to turn a corner here,'" Marcy says. "I decided I had to research something that I really cared about, something that was important to me." Marcy thought back to those nights on the roof of his house and the sheer happiness he felt gazing at the planets with his telescope. Could he connect that joy to a question that astronomers hadn't answered yet? Marcy remembered that when he was a boy, he had always wondered if the universe had other planets like Earth—planets that might harbor life.

That was it. Marcy decided to hunt for planets.

"But first," Marcy says, "I had to figure out a way for astronomers to detect extrasolar planets." He went straight to work. Within a few weeks he had sketched the basic detection method he uses today.

In 1994, Marcy married Susan Kegley, an expert

on chemical pollution. Marcy and Kegley love the outdoors, especially hiking and camping.

Marcy plays tennis every day, even when he's at the observatory hunting for planets. He also cheers for the UC Berkeley tennis team, and team members take the astronomy class he teaches about the planets. "I'm a wildly fanatical tennis player," Marcy says.

Today, Marcy is an astronomer at UC Berkeley and San Francisco State University. He enjoys teaching, but he loves planet hunting even more. The possibility of finding a planet like Earth keeps Marcy's gaze glued to the stars. "Finding a planet is discovering something no person has ever known. It's better than Columbus finding America, the New World. These planets are entire worlds. Some day we might be able to travel there. Who knows what we might find?"

*Marcy's dream of finding extrasolar planets came true. Here, a planet forming around the star CoKu Tau 4 might look like Saturn did billions of years ago.*

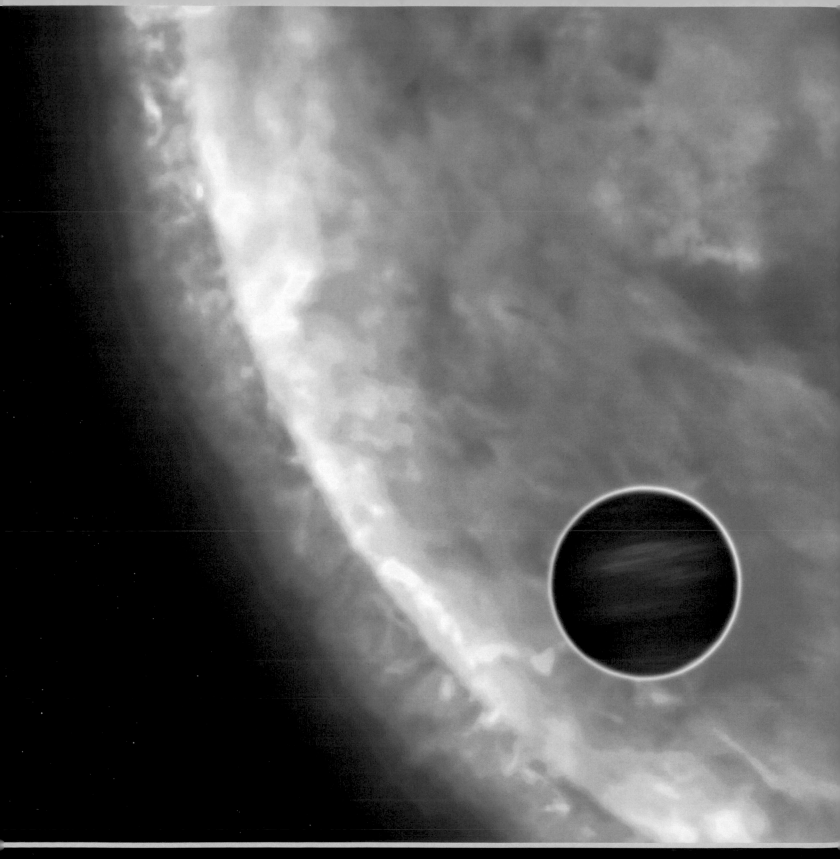

*In this artist's interpretation, a Jupiter-size planet is crossing in front of its parent star.*
*So far, most of the planets detected have been the size of Jupiter or larger.*

# THREE

## How to Find a Planet

In the telescope control room at Keck Observatory's headquarters in Waimea, Marcy checks the various computer screens. "Almost ready to start, Jason," he says into the microphone to McIlroy, the technician at the summit. Marcy watches McIlroy on the video screen mounted above the computers.

"Let's take a shot of the sky and see if it's dark enough," Marcy adds. He wants only pure starlight to enter the telescope.

"Right," McIlroy says. In the video screen, he nods.

Marcy settles into a swivel chair in front of the four main computers. "Anyone can have a telescope," he says, "but not everyone has a spectrometer."

A telescope alone, even one as powerful as the Keck I, cannot detect a planet outside our solar system. From Earth, a star's light is so bright that it washes out the light from a planet.

"Think of a searchlight on top of a lighthouse,"

## Wobble, Wobble, Little Star

So how does Marcy find a planet if he can't see it? He uses a Doppler spectrometer. If a planet is orbiting a star, the star will wobble as it is pulled by the gravity of the planet. Depending on where the planet lies in its orbit around the star, the star will be tugged either toward Earth or away from it.

"A planet's like a frisky dog being walked by its owner, the star," Marcy says. "For a star and its planet, the leash is gravity. You can figure out how large the planet is—its mass—by how much the star wobbles. You can also figure out the planet's speed, or velocity. The bigger the planet, the faster the star gets yanked around."

A spectrometer reveals a star's wobble by recording the changes in its light waves. Light shining from a star, like all light, travels in waves. All white light, including starlight, is made up of the visible colors of light mixed together. The colors of a rainbow—red, orange, yellow, green, blue, indigo, and violet—are known as the visible spectrum, and they always appear in this order because of the lengths of their waves.

The longest visible wavelengths are red. The wavelengths of orange, yellow, and so on become increasingly shorter. Violet has the shortest visible wavelength. When scientists talk about the wavelengths of light, they often refer to the "blue end" and the "red end" of the spectrum.

When light waves pass through something transparent, such as glass or water, the light slows down. When the speed decreases, the light bends, or refracts. If the light is bent sharply enough, as in a prism, the colors split apart from one another. Red light waves bend the least, followed by orange, then yellow, and so on. Violet light waves bend the most. When the waves bend and the colors split from one another, we see all the colors of the rainbow, or spectrum.

## Doppler Effect

The Doppler effect is named after Christian Doppler, an Austrian physicist. He noticed the change in light waves when a light source, such as a star, moves toward or away from an observer, such as an astronomer on Earth. Sound waves also produce Doppler shifts. Listen carefully the next time you hear an ambulance pass by. The *EEEEEEowww* of a siren is shrill as the ambulance zooms closer and the sound waves are compressed. The pitch lowers as the ambulance passes and the sound waves are stretched out.

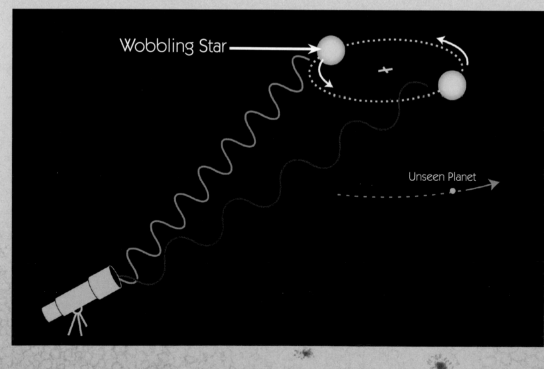

Wobbling Star

Unseen Planet

*When starlight enters the telescope, the spectrum reveals a shift toward blue or red, depending on whether the star is moving toward Earth (blue) or away from it (red). The blue waves of light are compressed. The red are stretched out.*

In a spectrometer, a device similar to a prism collects starlight through the telescope and separates it into a spectrum. Waves of starlight change depending on whether the star is moving away from or toward Earth. If the star is moving toward Earth, the waves are compressed and shift toward the blue end of the spectrum. Green light may look blue, for example, or orange light might look yellow. When the star moves away, the light waves are stretched out and shift toward the red end of the spectrum. Orange light may turn red, or blue light may look green. These changes in color are called Doppler shifts. Over time, a series of alternating redshifts and blueshifts indicate that a planet is causing the star to wobble.

## Spectral Fingerprints

But how can you tell you are looking at yellow light that has been blueshifted to green? How do you know it wasn't green all along?

Look for a spectral fingerprint.

Each type of gas has its own effect on light. When white light passes through a gas, such as hydrogen, the atoms and molecules that make up that gas absorb some wavelengths of light. The rest of the light passes through. If the light then passes through a device that reveals its spectrum, such as a prism or spectrometer, the colors will contain a pattern of black lines called absorption lines—a line of missing color for each wavelength that the gas absorbed. Each type of gas gives a different pattern of lines, like a fingerprint that identifies that gas.

When astronomers find a spectral pattern

that matches a gas, they know that the light passed through that kind of gas. If that pattern is also in the *wrong place* in the spectrum (too far toward the blue end or the red end), then they also know that the light has undergone a Doppler shift.

In 1983, when Marcy first conceived of his planet-hunting method, he already knew a lot about Doppler shifts and spectral patterns because he had used a spectrometer for his Ph.D. research. Using this technique to measure the wobble of a star, however, was a difficult challenge: starlight shifts are tiny and extremely hard to observe. Also, a star's spectrum has no built-in scale or ruler—no way to measure the small change in color.

In the 1970s, Gordon Walker and Bruce Campbell from the University of British Columbia figured out a way to measure the Doppler shifts of starlight by adding a gas into the spectrometer, but their technique wasn't precise enough to detect a planet. Marcy and Butler knew that the success of their technique lay in finding a different gas—exactly the right gas—to add to the starlight before it passes into the spectrometer. After a lot of experimenting, Marcy and Butler further developed Walker and Campbell's technique. Eventually, Paul Butler found the key: iodine gas.

## The Iodine "Ruler"

In the observatory on the summit, a sealed glass container filled with iodine gas is added into the telescope beam. Unlike gases that are highly explosive and dangerous, iodine is relatively stable and safe. Iodine also absorbs light at thousands

*Under a microscope, the iodine spectrum resembles a colorful product bar code. The dark absorption lines mark specific colors (wavelengths of light) that iodine gas absorbs. Similar to a fingerprint, the spectrum of iodine is a pattern of absorption lines that are always the same. Scientists use them like a ruler to measure the redshifts and blueshifts of starlight.*

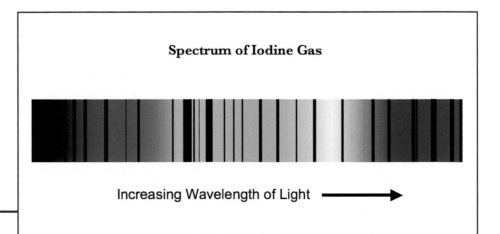

**Spectrum of Iodine Gas**

Increasing Wavelength of Light ⟶

Marcy sits in front of the three most important computers, working from a script of stars he plans to observe. The middle computer controls the optics of the Doppler spectrometer and the input of the iodine gas. The computer at the right records the spectra. The third computer (left) controls the camera-like device that snaps images of the spectra and stores them.

of different wavelengths, creating a distinct and recognizable pattern across the spectrum.

As the starlight enters the telescope, passes through the iodine, and goes into the spectrometer, the computer captures a combined spectrum of the starlight and the iodine. Marcy compares the combined spectrum with a spectrum of iodine alone. He uses the lines in the iodine spectrum like marks along a ruler, showing the positions of many known wavelengths. Those lines show how far the lines of other gases from starlight are out of place—how far they have been shifted toward red or blue. "The iodine gas is stationary at our telescope, so it has no Doppler shift. It's like using a ruler, but the ruler is the iodine spectrum, a spectrum we already know," Marcy says.

"See right there?" Marcy points to the computer screen on the far right. "That's our first star in the telescope. Jason's focusing on it now." Marcy points the cursor to a box on the computer screen and clicks the mouse. "Jason," Marcy says into the microphone, "I'm adding the iodine, so adjust the focus accordingly."

"Will do," McIlroy says.

Marcy uses a powerful spectrometer, known as the High Resolution Echelle Spectrometer (HIRES). It was built by a former member of the team, Dr. Steven Vogt, an astronomer at the University of California, Santa Cruz. Vogt continually improves and updates the spectrometer. The spectrometer at Keck is housed in a small room with steel walls, located next to the telescope's mirrors.

The spectrometer is located to the right of the telescope, in the room with the door. The room is as big as a living room, about twenty by twenty feet, and is sealed to keep out dust and moisture. The room maintains a steady temperature of 32 degrees Fahrenheit (0 degrees Celsius).

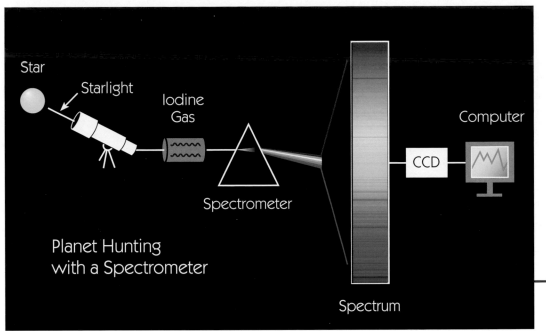

Planet Hunting
with a Spectrometer

*Starlight travels through the telescope and passes through a glass cylinder of iodine gas. The light continues through the spectrometer, which separates the light into a spectrum that shows patterns of both the gases around the star and the iodine in the cylinder. The spectrum is photographed by a device similar to a charge-coupled-device (CCD) light detector in a digital camera. A computer then stores and analyzes the image.*

*These spectra of starlight show the small Doppler shifts that occur during one complete orbit of a star.*

"The spectrometer works kind of like a digital camera," Marcy explains. "It takes a snapshot of the spectrum of light and records it."

Marcy points to a computer screen at the far left. "This computer controls the exposure time. It's like the control panel on a camera. Smaller stars, which give off less light, need longer exposure times than larger stars." He points to another screen just to the right. "And here's where all the spectrometer data is recorded. I'll take this back with me to UC Berkeley, where we'll analyze it."

Marcy flips through a sheaf of papers stapled together. This is his script of the stars he'll observe tonight. "I've got the whole night planned out here, scene by scene," he says.

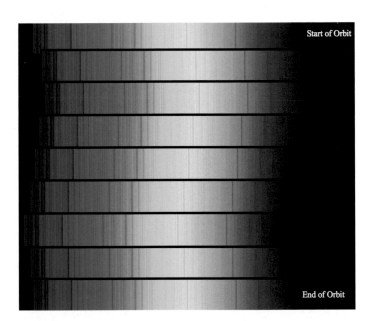

Start of Orbit

End of Orbit

*Debra Fischer observes a spectrum of starlight in the control room at Lick Observatory. An actual spectrum is several feet wide. The charge-coupled-device (CCD) light detector shrinks the spectrum and stacks the different wavelengths of light so the spectrum can be seen and analyzed on a standard-size computer monitor. The colors shown are false, but they represent the true range of red to blue colors in the spectrum.*

Marcy has spent hundreds of hours selecting the stars. Currently, he is interested in about two thousand of them. Tonight, he will focus on eighty stars that he has been following for years. Although Marcy hunts for all kinds of extrasolar planets, he's most passionate about this group of stars—these are the ones he thinks are most likely to harbor Earth-like planets. Why has Marcy chosen these stars? One reason is that they are relatively quiet and stable. They don't have solar flares, and they aren't expanding or pulsating, which would make a wobble difficult to detect.

## M Dwarfs: Little Stars with Big Promise

"See that star right there in the telescope?" Marcy points to the computer screen on the far right. "Not only is this star stable, but it's a little star, too. I'm wild about little stars. These stars offer an extraordinary chance to detect Earth-like planets."

Many stars have just one-tenth the mass of our Sun. Astronomers call these stars M dwarfs. Luckily for planet hunters, M dwarfs are the most prevalent kind of stars in the sky. "These little stars show off their planets more easily because they get tossed and pulled so much," Marcy explains. "It's like a dog owner that's only a six-year-old child. That six-year-old gets yanked around a lot more by a German shepherd than a big adult would."

Another reason Marcy likes little stars like M dwarfs involves a bit of luck. Sometimes when an astronomer is observing a star, a planet might happen to cross in front of the star, blocking the star's light. This is known as a transiting planet. If the star is big, a planet as small as Earth would be hard to find; it would hardly block any of the star's light. But if the star is little, an Earth-size planet would block a larger portion of the star's light—and astronomers might spot it.

*This densely packed ball of stars, known as globular cluster NGC 6397, lies in the constellation Ara. Scientists think globular clusters may date from before the formation of Earth's galaxy, the Milky Way. The reddish stars are very old. The hottest stars are blue. Stars are classified from hottest to coldest, along with other important characteristics, such as their mass and brightness. M dwarfs are the most common stars.*

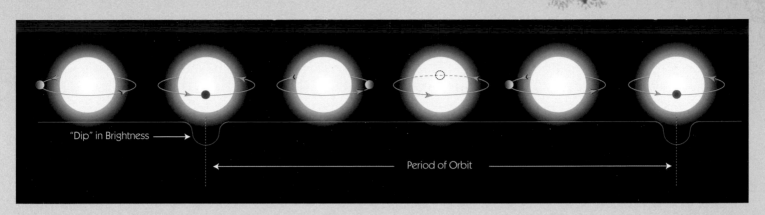

"Dip" in Brightness ⟶

⟵ Period of Orbit ⟶

Dr. David Charbonneau at Harvard University uses the transit method to hunt planets. He searches for stars that periodically dim as their planets pass across them. Charbonneau has detected four giant extrasolar planets using this technique.

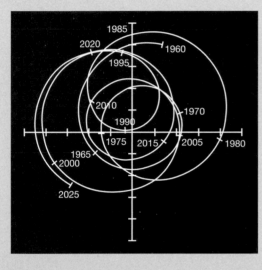

Using a technique called astrometry, astronomers have plotted the changing position of the Sun from 1960 to 2025. Like Doppler spectroscopy, astrometry detects planets by observing the wobble of a star. But instead of studying the Doppler shift of the star's light waves, astrometry measures the side-to-side movement of the star. With the discovery of the planet VB 10 b in May 2009, Steven Pravdo and Stuart Shaklan from NASA's Jet Propulsion Laboratory became the first to use this technique to detect an extrasolar planet. In the future, NASA's Space Interferometry Mission (SIM) will be equipped for astrometry.

Dr. David Bennett from the University of Notre Dame uses a technique called microlensing to detect planets. If, by chance, a star with planets passes between the telescope and a distant star, the light from the distant star (a), called the source star, bends around the star with planets (b), called the lens star. The gravitational influence of the lens star and its planet magnifies the light from the source star. As the planet (c) revolves around the lens star, it changes the qualities of the gravitational lens. By observing the brightening of the source star, astronomers can sometimes detect the lens star's planet. Using microlensing, Bennett's team has detected one of the smallest planets discovered so far, MOA-2007-BLG-192L b. It's only 3.3 times more massive than Earth.

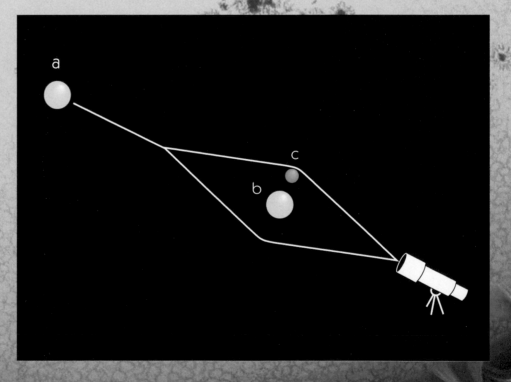

25

So far, no Earth-like planets have been detected using the transit method.

Little stars such as M dwarfs have one more benefit—they aren't as bright as our Sun. In fact, they are one-hundredth the brightness of the Sun. This dim light is a big plus if you're looking for habitable planets like Earth. Here's why.

Habitable planets are located in what astronomers call the habitable zone, also dubbed the "Goldilocks zone," which is the area around a star where conditions are "just right" to sustain life. One of these conditions is liquid water. Water is essential for life as we know it. On rocky planets, water can gather in pools and seas, mixing and transporting the necessary chemicals for life.

If a planet lies too close to a star, as Mercury does in relation to our Sun, the heat from the star will evaporate the water. If the planet lies too far

## Planets and Moons in the Goldilocks Zone

Many scientists think that life cannot exist without water. The temperature is important because it determines whether any water on a given planet would be in liquid form. On Earth, the atmosphere traps heat and keeps the planet warm. This is known as the greenhouse effect. But even a planet or moon in the habitable zone may not be habitable. Pollution added to the atmosphere can increase the greenhouse effect, making a planet too hot for life. In our solar system, the Moon lies in the habitable zone, but it is not habitable—it has no atmosphere to trap the Sun's heat. The daylight side of the Moon is brutally hot and the night side is freezing cold. Any water would evaporate or freeze.

*The green area marks the habitable zone around the star 55 Cancri, a region where planets might be able to sustain life. Scientists think that at least one planet in this system may lie in the habitable zone.*

away, as Mars does, the water will freeze. "It's kind of like a campfire," Marcy explains. "If the campfire is flickering and not giving off much heat, you have to move in closer to warm up. So an Earth-like planet, in order to be habitable, has to be very close to these little stars."

Planets that lie close to M dwarfs also can more easily yank on the star and cause it to wobble. It just so happens, then, that the closest planets are both the most detectable *and* the most likely to be habitable, so long as they lie in the habitable zone. Or as Marcy puts it, "They're crazy perfect."

Over the next three nights, Marcy will page through his script, taking measurements of the same eighty stars. Perhaps after reviewing the new data, he will pare down his search to even fewer stars for his next visit. Maybe in this special group lies an Earth-like planet waiting to be discovered.

## The Requirements for Life

On Earth, life requires three conditions: elements that can combine to form organic molecules, liquid water, and energy. The most important element is carbon, and it's found throughout the universe. Carbon is critical because it bonds with many other elements to form the molecules of life, such as nucleic acids (the building blocks of DNA and RNA) or amino acids (the building blocks of proteins). DNA contains the instructions for life. RNA builds proteins according to those instructions. Proteins carry out the tasks that make living cells function.

Liquid water is important because it serves as a place where all the substances that life needs can be transported, dissolved, and mixed. Many scientists think liquid water is so crucial that the search for extraterrestrial life essentially is a search for water.

Energy drives the chemical and biological reactions that sustain organisms. Life taps into many forms of energy, such as sunlight or heat that escapes through openings on the ocean floor, known as hydrothermal vents.

But these requirements for life are based on what we know about Earth. Life on other planets might be completely different.

*Some of the earliest-known forms of life on Earth were trilobites, small, hard-shelled creatures that lived millions of years ago and became extinct long before the first dinosaurs walked the planet. This fossil is a* Leonaspis *trilobite from Morocco. Scientists think it lived from 416 to 359 million years ago.*

*The large planet in the foreground is the fifth planet detected around the star 55 Cancri, which is similar to the Sun. The planet is about forty-five times the mass of Earth and completes an orbit in 260 days. The other four planets detected in this planetary system are seen orbiting closer to the star.*

# FOUR

## Discovering the First Extrasolar Planets

Lick Observatory
Mount Hamilton, California

"When I told people I was hunting for extrasolar planets, they would look down at their shoes, shuffle their feet, and change the subject," Marcy says. "They didn't take me seriously." During the 1990s, most scientists thought that detecting planets around other stars was impossible. What chance did Marcy, a relatively unknown astronomer with little financial support for his research, have of finding them?

So Marcy and Butler worked quietly together, usually at Lick Observatory on Mount Hamilton, California, near San Francisco State University, where Marcy was a professor and Butler was a graduate student. They spent many hours designing a method for detecting large planets like Jupiter. These planets would create bigger Doppler shifts than Earth-size planets would. The astronomers planned to hunt for giant planets first, then look for smaller ones

## Planet Formation

Planets form out of the disks of dust and gas that spin around new stars through a process known as core accretion. The spinning mass, called a protoplanetary disk, flattens out like a pancake and flings the dust outward from the star. Over time, some of the dust particles clump together into chunks of rock. The chunks collide and stick until they grow to the size of cities many miles across. These giant boulders continue to collide and eventually become the rocky cores of planets. Massive gas planets like Jupiter form far out in the disk, about five to ten times the distance that Earth is from the Sun, whereas smaller, rocky planets like Earth form closer to the star. The rocky cores of planets like Jupiter grow so big that their gravity attracts the hydrogen and helium gas that lie nearby in the disk. These gases add to the mass of the planet.

as they improved their methods. At that time, scientists predicted that such large planets would orbit far from their stars, at least three to four times as far as the Earth is from the Sun. Since Jupiter takes more than eleven years to orbit the Sun, Marcy and Butler figured they would need at least ten years of data to detect the full orbit of a large planet. They also confined their observations to a list of nearby stars about the same size as the Sun—stars they thought had the best chance of having planets.

The two men worked day and night for more than eight years, accumulating star spectra. They also designed computer software to analyze the Doppler shifts. Creating the software was challenging—the program had to be good enough to detect the Doppler shift with a precision of 1/1,000 of a pixel on the digital camera that records the spectra. When he was frustrated, Marcy often thought back to the advice he received from a professor in college, who encouraged him to keep going even when the task seemed impossible.

Steven Vogt, the astronomer who designed HIRES at Keck, also built and refined the spectrometer at Lick Observatory in Santa Cruz, California, where Marcy and Butler first conducted their observations. Vogt helped the men learn to focus and adjust the Lick instrument.

## Early Detections

While Marcy and Butler were refining their planet-hunting technique, two exciting events occurred. First, in 1992, Dr. Alex Wolszczan, a radio astronomer at Pennsylvania State University, detected three planets orbiting a pulsar. Pulsars are old stars that have burned out or exploded. They spin unusually fast and give off strong spurts of radioactive light. Wolszczan's discovery, though, still didn't answer the question whether planets orbited ordinary stars like our Sun.

Then in 1995, Dr. Michel Mayor and Dr. Didier Queloz, two astronomers at the Geneva Observatory in Switzerland, announced the discovery of the first planet orbiting an ordinary star: 51 Pegasi b. Mayor and Queloz happened upon the planet accidentally while measuring Doppler shifts in the light from 51 Pegasi to detect small, dark objects known as

### How Small Are the Doppler Shifts of Starlight?

The tiny Doppler shift of starlight can be compared to the shift in wavelengths of sound between half notes on a piano. Marcy's software is so precise that it detects Doppler shifts in starlight equivalent to one-millionth of the difference between the wavelengths of the musical notes C (shown above with the left hand) and C sharp (shown with the right hand).

brown dwarfs, which are smaller than ordinary stars but bigger than large planets.

This newly discovered planet was unlike anything astronomers had ever seen. It zooms around its star in only four days—an incredibly short year. Also, the planet's orbit and size are different from planets in our solar system. The planet is larger than Saturn, but its distance from its star is only one-seventh the distance between Mercury and our Sun.

Marcy wondered, Were Mayor and Queloz mistaken? Armed with their computer program and spectrometer, Marcy and Butler set to work. The men didn't have their own measurements for 51 Pegasi. So they furiously collected and analyzed their own Doppler shifts for the star. In just a few days, they confirmed Mayor and Queloz's finding: as strange as it seemed, there was indeed a planet.

"We were stunned and ecstatic," Marcy says. "The first extrasolar planet had been found."

*Michel Mayor and Didier Queloz discovered 51 Pegasi b, the first extrasolar planet known to orbit an ordinary star. In this painting, the sizes of the star and its planet (the red object near the middle) are shown in comparison with the sizes of Jupiter and Earth.*

*Within a few weeks of discovering their first planet, 47 Ursae Majoris b, Marcy and Butler detected a second, 70 Virginis b, shown here. This Jupiter-size planet may have massive moons that lie in the habitable zone. If so, the moons may have liquid water. In this painting, one of the planet's moons is shown resembling Earth.*

## "Normal" Planets Do Exist

By this time, Marcy and Butler had accumulated more than eight years of Doppler measurements. But they didn't have computers that were powerful and fast enough to analyze the complicated data. Finally, they acquired several computers that could do the work. "Now, with our own data in hand, we were ready to go," Marcy says.

Could there be evidence of a second planet hidden in the unanalyzed data? Once again, the two astronomers set to work, cranking out the results on their new computers. They pored over the spectra from hundreds of observations.

"There wasn't just one more planet—but two!" Marcy says. Only one month after Mayor and

Queloz's discovery, Marcy and Butler announced the detection of a planet orbiting star 47 Ursae Majoris (47 Ursae Majoris b) and one orbiting star 70 Virginis (70 Virginis b).

What made these findings especially thrilling was that they appeared to be somewhat more "normal" than the planet detected around 51 Pegasi. It takes months, not days, for these planets to orbit their stars. They also lie farther away from their stars.

Within one month's time, the known stars having planets had jumped from one (our Sun) to four. Stars with planets were no longer so rare. Suddenly, the idea of other solar systems was confirmed, and the notion of other planets teeming with life was possible.

Seemingly overnight, Marcy and Butler became the celebrities of planet hunting. But they didn't stop working. By 2000, only five years later, the two men had detected 60 extrasolar planets. Nine years later, their team had played a key role in discovering 180. The years Marcy and Butler had spent perfecting their techniques paid off. Other astronomers joined the race, finding about 220 more.

## Milestone Discoveries

In 1999, the team spotted the first "family" of planets, three planets orbiting the star Upsilon Andromedae. Finally, astronomers had proof of other solar systems comparable to our own.

In 2002, Marcy and Butler detected 55 Cancri d, the first large gas planet similar to Jupiter. The planet orbits about the same distance from 55 Cancri as Jupiter lies from the Sun. This finding is significant, because of two factors that scientists think made life possible on Earth.

The first is Jupiter's role in sheltering Earth from asteroids. "Because it's so big, Jupiter is a large cosmic vacuum cleaner, sucking up comets and asteroids," Marcy explains. "Without Jupiter, impacts would likely have destroyed life on Earth."

The second is that Earth orbits in the Sun's habitable zone. Years earlier, Marcy and Butler had detected two other planets (55 Cancri b and c) orbiting closer to the star 55 Cancri. A large gap, though, existed between these two planets and the newly discovered Jupiter-size planet. That gap was smack in the middle of the habitable zone. Could a rocky planet with water be orbiting in this gap?

If so, the 55 Cancri planetary system would have two features similar to our own solar system: a Jupiter-like planet and an Earth-like planet. And there might be life.

In November 2007, Marcy, Butler, Debra Fischer, and their team detected one more planet (55 Cancri f) squarely in this gap. However, Marcy believes that, unlike rocky Earth, this recently discovered planet is a gas giant similar to Jupiter. But it's possible that the planet has a rocky moon, which would also lie in the habitable zone. In our own solar system, scientists are researching the possibilities of

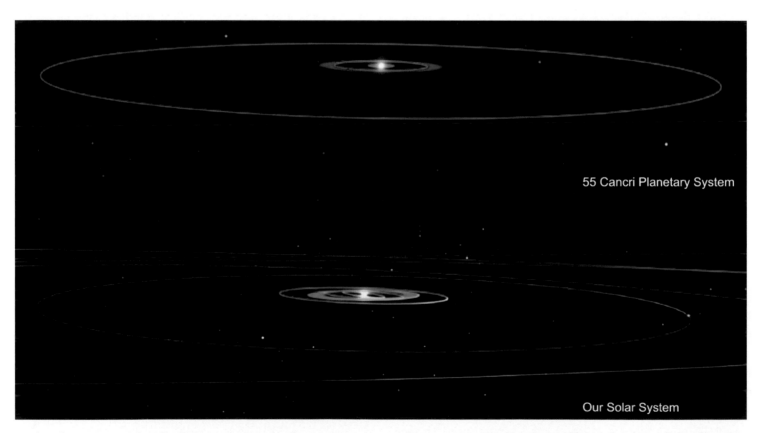

55 Cancri Planetary System

Our Solar System

*So far, the 55 Cancri family of planets (top) is the planetary system most like our own. The blue lines indicate the orbits of the planets. The 55 Cancri system may have more planets, perhaps rocky ones currently too small to detect in the habitable zone (green). If so, these planets and their moons (if they exist) could have life.*

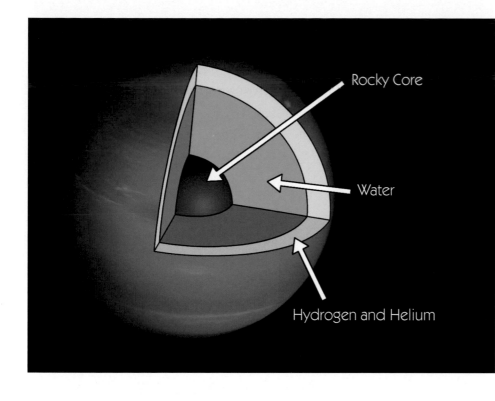

The density of Gliese 436 b suggests that the planet has a rocky center surrounded by an ocean of water. Hydrogen and helium form a thin layer around the planet.

life on several moons. A moon in the gap near 55 Cancri f might have water, and possibly life.

Marcy continues to focus his observations on the habitable zone around 55 Cancri, hoping to find more planets. If Earth-like planets do lie in the gap, though, they may be too small to detect using a Doppler spectrometer—at least for now.

The discovery of 55 Cancri f was significant for another reason, too—it brought the total number of detected planets orbiting 55 Cancri to five. (55 Cancri e was codiscovered in 2004 by several astronomers, including Marcy, Butler, and Fischer.) So far, this is the largest family of planets discovered and the planetary system most like our own.

The smallest planet Marcy and Butler have detected so far orbits the star Gliese 876. Spotted in June 2005, this planet (Gliese 876 d) is only 5.9 times more massive than Earth. Although astronomers aren't sure whether the planet is rocky, they think its small size means it isn't a gas planet like Jupiter.

## What Kind of Planet Is It?

In most cases, astronomers can't say for certain whether a specific planet is made of gas or rock or if it has water. Instead, they presume certain characteristics based on the planet's mass by comparing it with planets in our own solar

system. In May 2007, however, a unique set of circumstances helped Marcy and his team determine the composition of a planet.

A Belgian astronomer, Michael Gillon, was monitoring the brightness of star Gliese 436 when he noticed that the star dimmed and brightened every two and a half days. The dimming was caused by a transiting planet (Gliese 436 b). As the planet crossed directly in front of the star, it blocked some of the star's light.

Marcy and Butler had discovered this planet earlier, in 2004. They knew its mass from using HIRES at Keck. It's the size of Neptune, about twenty-two times more massive than Earth. However, Gillon's finding that the planet transited provided valuable additional information.

By measuring the fraction of light still shining when the planet crossed in front of Gliese 436, astronomers were able to calculate the planet's diameter. Then, armed with both the planet's diameter and mass, they computed the density of the planet. Density is a measure of how much matter is in an object or substance—that is, how closely the atoms and molecules are packed together. A planet's mass divided by its volume equals the planet's density. The density calculation for Gliese 436 b revealed the planet's composition.

The planet's density is 1.6 grams per cubic

centimeter. That's denser than water (1 gram per cubic centimeter) and less dense than rock (5.5 grams per cubic centimeter).

"This can only mean one thing," Marcy explains. "The planet has a rocky core and a huge ocean of water around it, kind of like a peach. Now we have a pretty good picture of a planet without even taking a snapshot. Just by taking the Doppler shift and transit measurements, we've learned the planet's internal structure."

In September 2009, the Swiss astronomer Didier Queloz and his team figured out the density of a second rocky planet, CoRoT-7 b. Astronomers are still trying to determine if the planet is all rock and iron like Earth or has a rocky core surrounded by water. But as Marcy says, "It's an exciting discovery on the road toward habitable planets."

## Finding the Unexpected

Each new planet brings Marcy and his team closer to understanding the diversity of the universe. Initially, Marcy had expected to find planets and solar systems similar to our own. He also aimed the telescope only at stars like our Sun. Now he observes a variety of stars, especially smaller M dwarfs. The more he and his team hunt for planets, the more they learn about the wide range and behaviors of planets. Many have orbits that are much more eccentric, or oblong,

than the nearly circular orbits in our solar system. Other planets orbit two or more stars.

At first, scientists were baffled by early detections of massive gas planets, known as hot Jupiters, orbiting close to their stars. Now scientists think these planets formed in the outer regions of their solar systems, then migrated inward. "Some newly formed gas planets slog through the gas and dust, losing energy through a kind of friction," Marcy says. "This causes the planets to spiral inward, just as the water and dirt in a bathtub spiral down the drain."

Only 1 percent of all stars have hot Jupiters. "These are rare quirks," Marcy says. "Most Jupiter-like planets and other planets orbit at normal distances and farther from the star."

Recently, Michel Mayor and his team of astronomers detected the smallest extrasolar planet so far, orbiting Gliese 581. The planet (Gliese 581 e) is only 1.9 times the mass of Earth. Although the planet is too hot for life, Marcy thinks the discovery is important. It implies that the Milky Way is home to many more small-size planets.

"Science is most exciting when we find things we don't expect," Marcy says. "What's neat about learning about different kinds of extrasolar planets is that they always cast a spotlight right back on Earth. Why is Earth the way it is? Maybe there's only one planet like Earth. But the range of diversity we see makes us think that there must be at least some elementary forms of life on other planets in our universe."

*Sunrise on CoRoT-7 b would be quite different from sunrise on Earth, as shown in this artist's rendition.*

## Detecting the Atmospheres of Extrasolar Planets

Astronomer David Charbonneau and his team use the infrared spectrograph instrument on board NASA's orbiting Spitzer Space Telescope to analyze a planet's atmosphere. When a planet passes in front of a star, the spectrograph captures the combined spectrum of light from the star and a little of the star's light that passed through the planet's atmosphere on its way past the planet. When the star's spectrum is subtracted from the combined spectrum, the chemical fingerprints of the planet's atmosphere are visible.

"Once we find rocky worlds that might host life, we will search for oxygen," Charbonneau says. "The presence of oxygen might indicate biological activity on the planet's surface." The Hubble and Spitzer space telescopes have detected sodium, water, methane, carbon monoxide, and carbon dioxide in the atmospheres of extrasolar planets.

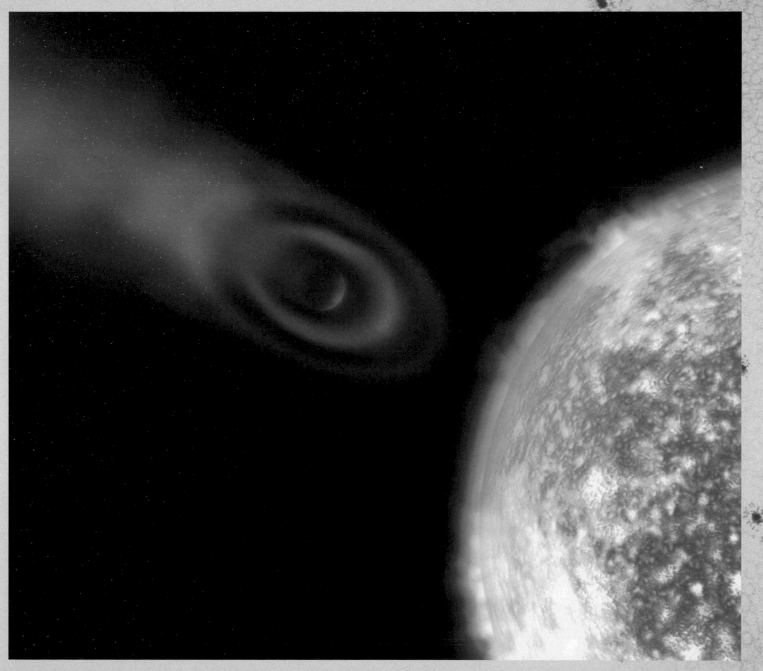

*In this artist's impression, the star HD 209458 blows carbon and oxygen off its planet, HD 209458 b.*

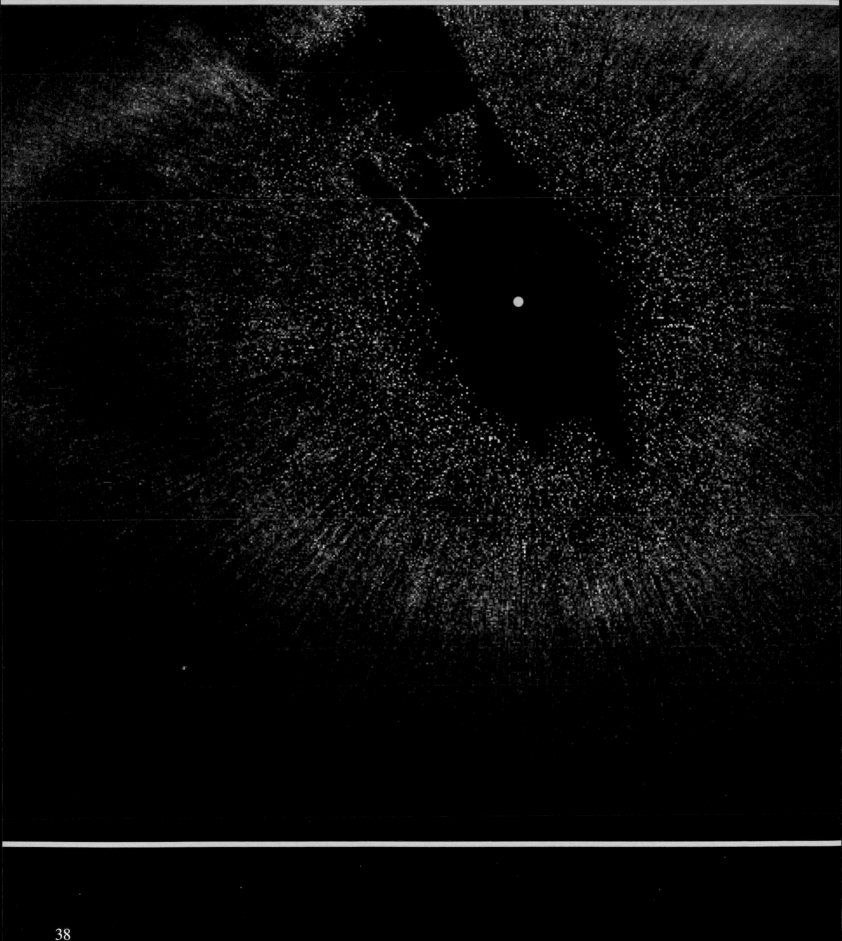

**Out-of-Sight Planets Now in View**

*For the first time, in November 2008, two teams of astronomers announced that they had photographed extrasolar planets. Dr. Paul Kalas and his team of astronomers from UC Berkeley photographed the planet Fomalhaut b, which orbits Fomalhaut. The photograph was made with a special camera on board the Hubble Space Telescope. The white dot in the center of the image is the star. Astronomers used an instrument called a coronagraph to block the star's light (the black area around the star), which made the planet visible. The small box (below) shows the planet. Astronomers compared images of the star taken in 2004 and 2006 and saw that a bright spot inside a huge dust ring had moved (inset, bottom right). It was a planet.*

*A second team of astronomers, led by Dr. Christian Marois of the Herzberg Institute of Astrophysics in Victoria, British Columbia, Canada, photographed a family of three planets orbiting star HR8799 with the Keck II and Gemini telescopes on Mauna Kea.*

## Fomalhaut b Planet

2006
2004

# FIVE

## The Next Generation of Planet Hunting

W. M. Keck Observatory, Hawaii

It is midnight in the control room at Keck Observatory's headquarters in Waimea as Marcy continues to hunt planets. This is the middle of his workday.

"Can you move the telescope west, Jason?" he asks the technician manning the telescope on the summit. He points to one of the computer screens. "See that? It's a binary star, one of two stars orbiting each other."

Marcy and Jason McIlroy discuss the exposure time for the star.

"We'll have to wait about ten minutes to get a good picture," Marcy says. "But even then it won't be as high quality as we want. We're starving for a stronger telescope, and this is the most powerful in the world."

*NASA's Kepler telescope (left) will track both Earth-size and larger planets that transit stars in or near the habitable zone. It is specially designed to catch the dimming and brightening of stars.*

*NASA's Space Interferometry Mission (below) will house an interferometer, an instrument that will gather light waves from a pair of telescopes, providing a wide-angle view of space.*

But Marcy doesn't have too long to wait for the next generation of planet-hunting techniques. NASA is launching new space telescopes and instruments that will be able to detect many more extrasolar planets—even planets as small as Earth. Launched in March 2009, NASA's Kepler Mission uses the transit method to detect planets. The telescope continuously takes pictures of the same one hundred thousand stars in the Cygnus constellation, hoping to record the dimming of starlight as planets pass in front of their parent stars. Marcy, a member of Kepler's science

## Is Anybody Out There?

In 1961, astronomer Frank Drake developed this equation to estimate the number of advanced civilizations in the Milky Way:

$$N = Rs \times Fp \times Np \times Fl \times Fi \times Fc \times L$$

Here's what the letters mean:
**N**—the number of technologically advanced civilizations in existence at any time
**Rs**—the rate at which stars form in the universe
**Fp**—the fraction of stars with planets
**Np**—the number of planets suitable for life
**Fl**—the fraction of planets where life takes off
**Fi**—the fraction of planets where intelligent life evolves
**Fc**—the number of civilizations that develops technology
**L**—how long an advanced civilization survives

Multiplied together, the seven factors on the right side of the equation equal **N**, the number of advanced civilizations. As scientists gain a greater understanding of each factor in the equation, **N** will more accurately predict extraterrestrial intelligence. Marcy's work as a planet hunter affects **Fp**, the fraction of stars with planets, and **Np**, the number of planets suitable for life.

Stars and planets are continually forming. Of the 200 billion stars in our Milky Way galaxy, Marcy estimates that about 20 billion have planetary systems, and about one-quarter of those probably have an Earth-like planet. That means there could be billions of planets in our galaxy ripe for life. If intelligent species live on only one in a million of those planets, then our galaxy would have thousands of advanced civilizations.

*At Arecibo Observatory in Puerto Rico, home to the world's largest radio telescope, scientists from the SETI Institute (Search for Extraterrestrial Intelligence) "listen" for radio waves from stars. These waves, if heard, might be signals from technologically advanced extraterrestrial civilizations. So far, no signals have been received. More than five million computer users at homes and in schools around the world volunteer their unused computer time to help analyze the telescope data through a program called SETI@Home. In June 2009, SETI's Project SERENDIP 5.5 updated the telescope's hardware to enable searches of a broader band of radio frequencies.*

*The surface of Venus is too hot for life as we know it. But does anything live in the Earth-like upper atmosphere?*

## Life on Alien Worlds?

What kinds of life might we find on extrasolar planets? Scientists called astrobiologists study the past, present, and future of life on Earth, in the solar system, and in the universe. They think extrasolar planets might be similar to some of the planets and moons in our own solar system that show signs of possible life.

Some of these worlds might have water, the most important requirement for life as we know it. On Mars, a planet that was similar to Earth billions of years ago, microscopic life might still flourish in underground hot springs or in permafrost, as it does on Earth. Gullies and dried-up lakes and rivers might contain fossils that could shed light on what life might have been like on Mars in the past. Life also might hide beneath the cracked, icy surface of Europa, a moon of Jupiter, where scientists believe there is an ocean over sixty miles deep. On Enceladus, a moon of Saturn, scientists think that jets of heat, vapor, and tiny ice particles blow out of cracks in the frigid moon.

Life also might thrive in more exotic habitats. On Venus, which is too hot and dry to be habitable on the surface or underground, bacteria might survive among the clouds. Titan, Saturn's largest moon, has huge lakes filled with flowing liquid methane and ethane. Instead of water, alien life may have emerged in these liquids, and still might thrive.

team, will use the Keck I telescope to verify the detected planets. He also will determine the planets' densities.

Planned for launch within the next ten years, NASA's Space Interferometry Mission (SIM) is the most powerful space-bound planet-hunting telescope so far.

As one of the leaders of the SIM science team, Marcy plays a key role in the mission's project to discover planets. "SIM is exciting because it will look for Earth-like planets around stars that are very close to Earth," Marcy says. "We'll be able to follow up with other telescopes and get clearer images and information. These are the stars we humans will be able to travel to in the next century."

Kepler and SIM are paving the way for more sophisticated missions in the future, such as the Terrestrial Planet Finder (TPF). TPF would be an array of telescopes designed to detect and photograph Earth-like planets. A spectrometer on TPF would analyze the atmospheres of the planets.

"TPF is beyond the horizon but will be the dream machine for characterizing the true properties and habitability of other rocky planets," Marcy says. "Any planet with an oxygen atmosphere and surface oceans will be a suspect for life from forty light-years away."

## Are We Alone?

Are we alone in the universe? For thousands of years, philosophers and scientists have pondered this question. Finally, we are on the verge of some answers.

"Now we know that the fundamentals of gravity, electricity, and physics are the same throughout the universe," Marcy says. "The building blocks of life—complex organic molecules—are everywhere, and water abounds. Life has been revealed as a natural wonder."

Meanwhile, scientists have designed space missions and robots to probe the planets and moons for habitable worlds. More than four hundred

*Kuahu Lele, a Hawaiian altar on top of Mauna Kea, was built on June 21, 1999, to celebrate the summer solstice. Many Hawaiians believe that* ho'okupu *(offerings) placed on the top of the wooden altar leap off into the heavens for the gods and goddesses. The altar is located amid an enclosure of silversword plants. These plants grow only on high mountains in Hawaii.*

extrasolar planets have been detected, and more will be discovered with new telescopes in space.

"One day, our grandchildren will send robotic probes and maybe even themselves to explore Earth-like planets," Marcy says. "Imagine finding another species that we can communicate with, that we can share our art, music, and literature with, and that might unite us as people."

Outside the Keck Observatory, on the summit of Mauna Kea, oddly shaped shadows darken the mounds of lava that dot the mountain. The night sky beckons. Mercury shines brightly above. Hundreds of twinkling stars look so big and close that it seems as if they might drop from the sky. Just as the ancient Hawaiians climbed to the top of Mauna Kea to connect to the heavens, Marcy and other astronomers will continue to travel to this remote spot in their quest to unravel the mysteries of the universe.

*Beyond the Milky Way lie tens of billions of other galaxies, many similar to NGC 1232 (above), a large spiral galaxy containing billions of stars and planets. The sheer number of galaxies, stars, and planets in the universe makes people question whether Earth is the only planet with intelligent life.*

# To Learn More

## Books

Aguilar, David A. *Planets, Stars, and Galaxies: A Visual Encyclopedia of Our Universe*. Washington, DC: National Geographic, 2007. An illustrated guide to the universe, including extrasolar worlds.

Jackson, Ellen. *Looking for Life in the Universe: The Search for Extraterrestrial Intelligence*. Boston: Houghton Mifflin, 2002. Astrophysicist Jill Tarter, the SETI Institute, and the search for alien life.

Miller, Ron. *Extrasolar Planets: Worlds Beyond*. Brookfield, CT: Twenty-First Century Books, 2002. The search for extrasolar planets, and illustrated descriptions of detected planets.

Nardo, Don. *The Search for Extraterrestrial Life*. San Diego, CA: Lucent Books, 2006. The hunt for extrasolar planets and alien life.

Skurzynski, Gloria. *Are We Alone? Finding Life in the Milky Way Galaxy*. Washington, DC: National Geographic Society, 2004. The quest for extrasolar planets, the study of astrobiology, and the search for extraterrestrial life. Includes interviews with key scientists.

Turner, Pamela S. *Life on Earth—and Beyond: An Astrobiologist's Quest*. Watertown, MA: Charlesbridge, 2008. Astrobiologist Chris McKay and his travels to extreme environments.

## Easy Reading

Halpern, Paul. *Faraway Worlds: Planets Beyond Our Solar System*. Watertown, MA: Charlesbridge, 2004. Illustrated book of extrasolar planets with explanations of planet detection methods.

## More Challenging Reading (High School and Above)

Casoli, Fabienne, and Thérèse Encrenaz. *The New Worlds: Extrasolar Planets*. Berlin; Springer, 2007. Illustrations and discussion of the hunt for extrasolar planets, detection methods, and the range of planets discovered.

Croswell, Ken. *Planet Quest: The Epic Discovery of Alien Solar Systems*. New York: Free Press, 1997. History of the discovery of planets, detection methods, and early planet discoveries.

Grady, Monica M. *Astrobiology*. Washington, DC: Smithsonian Institution Press, 2001. Detailed information and illustrations about astrobiology, alien life, and the search for Earth-like planets.

Lemonick, Michael D. *Other Worlds: The Search for Life in the Universe*. New York: Simon and Schuster, 1998. History of the search for extraterrestrial life and the detection of extrasolar planets. Includes interviews with key scientists.

## Web Sites*

Alien Earths
www.alienearths.org
Space Science Institute's interactive Web site on research and detection of extrasolar planets and alien life.

*Astrobiology Magazine*
www.astrobio.net
NASA astrobiology program magazine, featuring astrobiology updates and Web links, articles about extrasolar planets, NASA missions, and other space-related topics.

Kepler Mission
kepler.nasa.gov
Official Web site for the Kepler Mission's search for habitable planets.

Planet Quest: Exoplanet Exploration
planetquest.jpl.nasa.gov
Interviews with planet hunters, most recent planet discoveries, and links to multimedia resources and space missions.

SETI Institute
www.seti.org
Education, astrobiology, and research about the study of life in the universe and the search for extraterrestrial intelligence.

The Extrasolar Planets Encyclopaedia
www.exoplanet.eu
Daily update of extrasolar planet detections, catalog of discoveries and news releases, and links to ongoing and future planet searches.

The Planetary Society
www.planetary.org/exoplanets/index.php
A catalog of extrasolar planets, including notable discoveries, detection methods, and animations of each planet's orbit.

## For Educators

NASA Education
www.nasa.gov/audience/foreducators/5-8/index.html
Links to age-appropriate classroom activities and topics.

NASA's Heasarc: Education and Public Information
heasarc.gsfc.nasa.gov/docs/outreach.html
Education and outreach programs for students and teachers, classroom activities and lesson plans, and links to astronomy-related topics.

Planet Quest: Educator Resources
planetquest.jpl.nasa.gov/resources/resources_index.cfm
Links to resources about planet hunting and related fields.

*Active at time of publication

# Glossary

**absorption lines** microscopic black lines observed in a spectrum, where the chemical components of a gas have absorbed colors (wavelengths) of light.

**amino acid** an organic molecule that combines with others of its kind to form proteins. Proteins carry out tasks essential to life, such as building organs and digesting food.

**asteroids** pieces of rock and metal remaining from when the solar system formed. Asteroids orbit the Sun, and most lie between Mars and Jupiter in a region known as the Asteroid Belt.

**astrobiologist** a scientist from any of several fields who studies the past, present, and future of life on Earth, on other planets, and moons.

**astrometry** a method of planet hunting that relies on the side-to-side movement of a star across the sky.

**atom** the smallest particle of an element. Each atom is submicroscopic and is composed of a central part made of protons (and in most cases neutrons) and one or more electrons in orbit around the nucleus.

**brown dwarf** a small, dim star. Unlike other stars, a brown dwarf is not hot or large enough to emit light by fusing atoms together and forming new elements, a process known as nuclear fusion.

**charge-coupled device (CCD)** an electronic detector in a spectrometer that captures a spectrum of starlight and records the image as a series of dots, or pixels.

**comet** a chunk of ice, rock, and interstellar dust that orbits the Sun. As comets pass through the inner solar system and are heated by the Sun, they form long, bright tails of gases and dust that diffuse into space.

**core accretion** a process that occurs when dust particles and gas spinning around a new star collide and grow bigger, and begin to draw in the material around them, eventually forming the cores of rocky planets.

**coronagraph** an instrument attached to a telescope that blocks out the light from a star so that dimmer objects, such as extrasolar planets, may be seen.

**cubic centimeter** a unit of measurement of volume, in which the length of each side of a cube equals one centimeter.

**density** a measurement of the amount of matter in a given volume.

**diameter** the measurement of a straight line from one side of a circle or sphere through the center to the opposite side.

**DNA (deoxyribonucleic acid)** genetic material in a cell's nucleus that contains the instructions for the growth and development of a living thing.

**Doppler effect** or **shift** a change in the frequency of light or sound waves as an object moves toward or away from an observer.

**Doppler spectroscopy** a method for measuring the Doppler effect or shift of starlight by studying a star's spectrum.

**element** one of the hundreds of fundamental, naturally occurring substances that make up the physical universe. The smallest unit of an element is an atom with a characteristic number of particles called protons, electrons, and neutrons. One of the most important elements is carbon, because carbon atoms bond easily with one another and with other elements to form organic molecules, one of the requirements for life on Earth.

**extrasolar planet** a planet that orbits a star other than our Sun.

**galaxy** a collection of stars and interstellar matter joined together by gravity.

**gravity** the force of attraction that objects exert on one another. A star wobbles because of the pull of gravity exerted by its planet.

**greenhouse effect** the warming of a planet due to the atmosphere's ability to trap heat. On Earth, carbon dioxide in the atmosphere keeps our planet warm and habitable.

**habitable planet** a rocky planet having liquid water that orbits in the **habitable zone** of its star.

**habitable zone** the region around a star where an orbiting planet or moon might have liquid water.

**hydrothermal vents** openings in the ocean floor that spew super-hot water that is rich in minerals.

**interferometer** an Instrument that merges the gathered light from two or more telescopes.

**interstellar** of or relating to space in the midst of and surrounded by stars.

**light wave** the energy of light envisioned as an up-and-down or side-to-side oscillation similar to an ocean wave. Alternatively, light can be envisioned as a particle called a photon.

**mass** the quantity of matter in a given object.

**M dwarf** the smallest and most common type of star, also known as a red dwarf. They are much dimmer than stars like our Sun.

**microlensing** a method of detecting extrasolar planets in orbit around stars that happen to be positioned to act as lenses, magnifying the light of more distant stars. The presence of the planet is revealed by its effect on the magnifying properties of its sun.

**migration** the movement of a newly formed gas planet inward toward the star.

**Milky Way** the galaxy where Earth and its solar system are located.

**molecule** a group of atoms bound together. A molecule of water is composed of two atoms of hydrogen bound to one atom of oxygen.

**moon** any natural satellite of an object other than a star, especially a planet.

**Moon** Earth's natural satellite.

**nucleic acid** an organic molecule that makes up DNA and RNA.

**optical telescope** a telescope that collects and focuses visible light to magnify an image in the sky.

**organic molecule** a molecule containing carbon in long chains that chemically bond to atoms of other elements, such as hydrogen and oxygen. Organic molecules are found in living organisms and are essential for life on Earth.

**pixel** a small dot, also called a picture element. Pixels are combined to make images on video screens such as computers, digital cameras, and televisions.

**planet** a spherical body that orbits a star and is not large enough to be considered a star itself.

**planetary system** a group of planets, moons, comets, and other objects in orbit around a star. Earth and its planetary system are called the solar system.

**prism** a transparent object that bends light, breaking it into the colors of the rainbow.

**protoplanetary disk** a flattened disk of dust and gas that spins around a newly forming star. Eventually, planets form from the dust and gas.

**pulsar** a rotating neutron star that emits a regular pulse of electromagnetic energy. A neutron star is the densely packed remains of a dead star that has died out and exploded.

**radio telescope** a telescope used to study the radio waves emitted from stars and other objects.

**radio waves** light waves that are too long to be seen by the human eye and that can be detected by a radio receiver.

**RNA (ribonucleic acid)** nucleic acids that transmit the DNA's genetic instructions to cells and build proteins.

**solar flare** an explosion of gas in the atmosphere around the Sun or a star.

**spectrometer** an instrument that magnifies a spectrum so the image can be more readily observed.

**spectroscopy** the study of a body in space by observing its spectrum.

**spectrum** the pattern seen when something clear, such as a prism, splits white light into its component colors. The plural form of *spectrum* is *spectra*.

**star** a mass of gas that is held together by its own gravity and that glows as a result of its own heat.

**Sun** the star in our solar system.

**transiting planet** a planet that crosses between the Earth and a star.

**transit method** a means of detecting planets by observing the periodic dimming of a star. The star dims due to the passing of a planet between Earth and the planet's parent star.

**universe** all planets, moons, planetary systems, galaxies, interstellar bodies, matter, and energy that exist.

**velocity** the speed of an object's movement.

**visible spectrum** the colors of light that humans can see—red, orange, yellow, green, blue, indigo, and violet—and that form white light when mixed together.

**volume** an amount of space, such as the space that an object takes up, often measured in cubic centimeters.

# Index